Dr. J.L. Clayton

ORDER IN THE HOUSE
Walking in your gifts and callings

AB

ALTAR BOOKS
A DIVISION OF

QUIVERFULL
PUBLISHING

Strong, James. *Strong's Exhaustive Concordance of the Bible, (7th ed.).* Abingdon Press, 1890. Print.

Merriam-Webster.com. Merriam-Webster, 2011.

Paperback: ISBN-13: 978-1-7325276-5-2

ISBN-10: 1-7325276-5-2

ENDORSEMENTS

Bishop Clayton has applied sound scholarship and exhaustive research to make an important contribution to the ongoing conversation about church leadership, governance, and spiritual gifts. This is a must-read volume for those who would delve into the subject and it is a vital concern for all who are called to lead in Christ's church. I recommend this book without reservation.

The reader will find it well organized, clearly articulated, and thorough in examining both the obvious teachings of scripture as well as subtle nuances. Bishop Clayton gives special attention to language, context, and hermeneutic integrity in building and presenting his case. This is a very readable and compelling edition.

Tom Sims
CEO of 4141ministries.com
Director at Mid Valley School of Theology

Dr. J. L. Clayton's new book, "Order In The House", is a very powerful, thought provoking, and a much-needed word for such a time as this. It is full of biblical insights that will help you stay focused, as well as, alert on this Kingdom Journey!

Forever Remaining in His Presence,
Apostle Katrina M. Walker
Waldorf, Maryland

I am personally gratified that Dr. Clayton's book on *"Order in The House" Walking in Your Gifts and Callings"* has been now made available to the body of Christ. This is a must read. It is time for the Body of Christ to learn and accept that there is a proper way for the people of God to conduct themselves in the House of God, and as a witness of the Anointing of God. Dr. Clayton is truly a Teacher /Preacher of the Gospel and a man that has a heart for the people of God.

It is my desire that these teachings be treated with the respect it deserves.

Michael A. Smith Sr
Sr. Pastor,
True Light Community Church, Fresno Ca.

Dr. Clayton has captured the hearts of Leaders and parishioners with this amazing and thought-provoking book. Through this book his practical insight concerning the ministry gives one the ability to cast down governmental strongholds and issues that are currently operating in the church at large. And clearly through his eye-opening information regarding Gods government, order could easily be set back in the church so that we would function from a place of kingdom authority.

I have always known him as a very passionate man that wanted to empower the men/women of God so that we would operate from the perspective of kingdom authority and power. This book reveals Dr. Clayton profound spiritual insight that has captured the total essence of that passion and the fruit will be enjoyed by many.

I highly recommend this book to be used as a study guide to all ministers of the gospel. The information is food for the hungry soul and for the soul that want to be liberated and operate from a kingdom viewpoint.

Maria Davis
Senior Pastor, Healing Streams Community Church
Moreno Valley, California

INTRODUCTION

Government has been around since the beginning of time. Man has always had his way of attempting to govern himself. Throughout the history of mankind in every culture and on every continent, attempts have been made to create some form of governmental structure. In Ancient Egypt, there was a pharaoh. The word *pharaoh* translated from the Greek means *big house*. In Mesopotamia, the king of Babylon created a collection of ethics and laws called the Code of Hammurabi, which was the first written record of a standard. The code listed the virtues of the Mesopotamian society as well as the consequences of disobedience. In the ancient culture of Greece, the

Hellenistic peoples were instrumental in laying the foundation for Westernized democracy. The people of Kush had a matriarchal system of government where the queen ruled, which led to the system used in Great Britain today. Now, many of these systems have passed away, but God is eternal. So, in essence, God's government, or His way of doing things, has been around since *before* the beginning of time.

This book will focus on God's intent for His government and His kingdom as it relates to man, to situations on the earth, and to His church. As you read this book, it is my pleasure to help shed light on the gifts and callings of man in Scripture as they pertain to godly government. I desire to help you, the reader, understand the need for God's government within your personal life as well as within the church. My prayer is to aid in bridging the relationships among all who believe in Christ so that we independently and collectively discover who and what God has called us to do. I believe the church has been operating beneath God's perfect design, and while this book will touch only the tip of the iceberg, I trust this effort will bring a measure of revelation to the intricate detail of the order of God and deliver insight into understanding how the full government of God affects us, both as individuals as well as the corporate body of the church,

CONTENTS

Chapter 1

THE ORDER OF GOD

Webster's Collegiate Dictionary defines *government* as *the act or process of governing: moral conduct or behavior; the continuous exercise of authority over and the performance of functions for a specific group.*

Strong's Concordance provides us with an additional definition of government, coming from the Hebrew word *Misrah,* which means *empire.* This is derived from the word *Sarah,* which means *to prevail and to have power as a prince.* If we merge the definitions of both Hebrew words with what we find in *Webster's*

Collegiate Dictionary, we can conclude that Jesus then

is the

continuous authority exercising the order of God over His Kingdom as a prevailing prince.

Therefore, it becomes imperative for us to understand that when Isaiah 9:6 (KJV) says, *"And the government shall be upon his shoulders,"* according to this specific definition, Scripture is declaring that Jesus the Christ carries full authority concerning the order of God.

We must also understand that every king has his throne. The dynamics of a throne represent what a king can do from his throne; it is his place of operation. The book of Isaiah shows us four thrones.

Wonderful Counselor

Wonderful Counselor points us to the Messiah as King, who determines and carries out a programmed (determined) order. Isaiah 14:26-27 declares, *"This is the purpose that is purposed upon the whole earth: And this is the hand that is stretched out upon all the nations. For the Lord of hosts hath purposed, and who shall disannul it? Moreover, his hand is stretched out, and who shall turn it back?"* These Scriptures indicate that God had His own plan, His own purpose and government before the foundation of the world, and there is nothing anyone can do to upset His governing authority.

Mighty God

The phrase *Mighty God* signifies His divine power as a warrior. *Warrior* in the Hebrew is *gibbor,* meaning *powerful, tyrant, champion, chief, to excel, strong, giant.* The word *warrior* indicates not only that God's government will be powerful and strong, but also that God's order or His way of doing things will be champion over every other system of government and chief above all other authorities, and that it will continue to excel.

Everlasting Father

Everlasting Father expresses that He will be an enduring, compassionate provider and protector.

Isaiah 40:9-11 supports the fact that God's hand extends to His sheep as a shepherd and gently leads. God's hand or government can exemplify force and power, yet it yields to the gracefulness of nurturing while at the same time empowering His children to reach their place of purpose and destiny in His plan.

Prince of Peace

Prince of Peace reflects that His rule will bring wholeness and wellbeing to individuals and society. Isaiah 11:6-9 compares small things to great things as well as what may not be a threat to what is a threat. God indicates through that passage that it's not about avoiding what may prove to be difficult but relying on the knowledge of Christ, which is as

great as the

waters covering the sea. This shows that God's order and government cover everything that may concern us.

Understanding the term *government* and its function is essential to the personal growth and development of every believer. Within government, two sides work together to set and accomplish its purpose—a structural arm and an operational arm, each of which also serves an individual purpose. The structural arm represents the foundation and includes the permissive barriers for the operational arm. Neither branch is more necessary than the other, nor does one carry a greater responsibility; so, in effect, they are equal in nature. Neither can perform without the other. The operational arm is the functionality of the government. It carries out the thought and input of the structural arm.

For example, let's take the United States of America, a Democratic Republic. The forefathers established and laid the foundation for the structure. They created a Constitution and Legislative Branch, etc. Now, the Constitution would be an empty document if it were never executed, but the Constitution has become a living structural document for individuals to follow the parameters of its operational barriers. Likewise, the Congress and Senate would be void institutions without congressmen and senators who bring those positions to life.

If we parallel this same thought to the church and God's established government, we can see the source where man derived some, if not all, of his governmental structure and operations.

In 1 Corinthians 12:27, we see that God was establishing order in the church, but one cannot establish order absent of structure. God declares in the very next verse (12:28) that He has set some in the church that are first apostles, secondarily prophets, and thirdly teachers, and after those miracles.

In my study, I always wondered what the difference was between 1 Corinthians 12:28 was and Ephesians 4:11, if there were any. I questioned why the pastor and evangelist weren't listed.

As we evaluate 1 Corinthians 12:28, we see that God uses the word *set* rather than *give* or *gave*. That's because God was talking about the structure of the church, not its operation. He set apostles, which are foundational. He set prophets, who are the visionaries. He also set teachers, which are informational. God declares that after the structure has been built, then we can operate in miracles, gifts of healing, helps, governments, and diversity of tongues.

Before we go further, it's important to explain the difference between an office and a gift. In the church as a whole, we intertwine people that walk in offices with people that walk in gifts. Those who walk in offices have no choice in the matter, because offices are set positions such as apostle, prophet, teacher and pastor. We will discuss those offices individually a little later. When something has been set or established, the representation is that it's fixed and unmovable.

As an illustration, when you set something in a particular place where you want it, that's where you remember it being, and that's where it's supposed to be. If someone moves the object you have set somewhere, it causes imbalance, frustration and even confusion. That's why when God declares that He has placed these offices in the church, it is not our job to move or remove them. They are provided for the structure of the church, both globally and locally.

The latter part of 1 Corinthians 12:28 discusses the fact that there will be gifts of healings, helps, government and diversification of tongues. Verses 29 to 31 ask whether all are apostles, prophets, teachers or workers of miracles; it also asks whether all have the gifts of healing or whether all speak in tongues or interpret. Verse 31 urges us to *"covet earnestly the best gifts."* It is in these verses where we see for the first time that God includes the gifts of

the apostle,

prophet and teachers along with these other gifts. The gifts described here are different from the set offices of which He was speaking in verse 28. We discover in reviewing these verses that God had turned his attention to the operational function of government rather than the structure of it. The structure tells us what is, and the operation explains how we are going to accomplish what is.

Ephesians 4:11-12 says, *"And he gave some, apostles; and some, prophets; and some, evangelists; and some, pastors and teachers; For the perfecting of the saints, for the work of the ministry, for the edifying of the body of Christ."* The first part of this verse tells us how we are going to operate and accomplish our work in a godly

structure. Note the

language God uses at the beginning of this verse as compared to the language in 1 Corinthians 12:28. He says He *gave,* not *set.* So, this lets us know that He is talking about two different functions. To bring clarity, we see that 1 Corinthians is talking about called positions, set positions or positions of structure; but Ephesians is declaring gifted positions, positions of mobility and operations, positions of empowerment. What makes these positions vastly different is that the called positions have no choice while the gifted positions are given freely to all that want them.

The body of Christ will not begin to reach its fullness until those in the body begin to covet these gifts of operation. When we understand that, walking in an apostle gifting is indeed just merely walking in an apostolic nature. To walk in an apostolic nature means that, as the people of God, the gospel of Jesus Christ should always first and foremost be our foundation. This means we should live a life of order and kingdom fulfillment. This should not be an expectation of only clergy members. Children of God should always have a heart for God's governmental structure and operation in their personal life.

As we walk in the gifts of prophecy, we will be able to take God at His word and speak those things that are not as though they were. We will walk in the

simplest form of prophecy and take what has not

been received or manifested and prophesy it forth by the Word of God.

In the gift of a pastor, we should possess undying love for one another; we could walk in a spirit of restoration and care along with the willingness to cover our brother or sister and be their keeper.

The gifting of an evangelist has merely the heart to share the good news to those that don't believe and the ability to administer prayer, healing and deliverance to those in need.

Lastly, the teaching gift indicates that we all should be students of the Word, ready to give account at any moment about our faith. The Bible declares in 2

Timothy 2:15 that we need to study to show ourselves approved. You may ask, "Approved for what?" We need to be approved to teach and explain as well as exhort with clarity and understanding.

All these gifts were given to the body of Christ to become perfected, to do the work of the ministry so that the body can be edified. Unfortunately, we have perverted God's Kingdom and His way of doing things in that we have allowed only a few to operate in these gifts, therefore only a few have been edifying the body. These gifts were given for the whole body to be edified. The definition of *edify* is *to lift up, exhort, embrace, fulfill.* God wants this for the entire body. It is time that the body of Christ flowed

in true kingdom

order. God has unleashed the anointing into the body that we should covet these gifts and walk in them truly as God has ordained them to be used, so that we can come into the unity of the faith and knowledge of the Son of God, become a perfect man and walk into the measure of the stature of the fullness of Christ.

Chapter 2

APOSTLE

2 Timothy 3:16 indicates that all Scripture is inspired by God and is profitable for doctrine, for reproof, for correction, for instruction in righteousness (which can also be interpreted as the government of God) that the man of God may be perfect, thoroughly furnished unto all good works. That's why it becomes essential for us to look at the office of apostleship first in this series of delegated positions in the kingdom of God. Each position or office—apostle, prophet, evangelist, pastor—is a position held by men. For a man to become an

advocate in the kingdom-building process or the

flow

of church order, he has to be consumed with sound biblical doctrine and righteous instruction because only through these can he fulfill the obligations of kingdom concepts and the will of God for man.

The Greek word for *apostle* is *apostolos* which means *messenger, one sent, ambassador*. It comes from the word *apostello* which means *to be set apart on a mission or a delegate*. Clearly, the first thought of an apostle from these definitions would be one set apart for a mission (*apostello*) to be sent (*apostolos*) forth as an ambassador.

To understand the governing function of an apostle, we would need to understand that a church or another individual cannot send the apostle according to Scripture. Kingdom apostleship is bestowed only by God. Romans 1:4-5 indicates that we have received grace and apostleship through Jesus Christ. Matthew 10:1-2 declares that Jesus called His disciples, and out of them He named twelve apostles; Luke 6:13 also states that Jesus called His disciples and out of them He chose twelve He named apostles. This is different from being sent by a church, person or denomination. In Acts 13:2-4 we see that Barnabus and Saul were being sent out to do the work that God had called them to do. Verse three explains that, *"They sent them away,"* and verse four declares, *"Being sent forth by the Holy Spirit, they departed."* In verse 3 *sent* is the Greek word *apoluo*,

which means *release.* The example

in verse four means *sent away*. Neither supports the thought of apostleship. Indeed, an apostle is sent by one in solemn authority (Jesus Christ) because the government is on His shoulder. Men operate only out of delegated authority within the scope of the office that they are assigned. Jesus uses the office of the apostle to facilitate His continuous authority over the body of Christ. According to 1 Corinthians 12:28, the office of the apostle was established and implemented by Christ, not man.

In the previous chapter, we established that God saw fit to place the apostle first rather than any other office. From this, we can see that the office is

considered foundational and the other offices sit

upon it. Ephesians 2:20 states that Christ Himself is the Chief Cornerstone, indicating that even though the apostle is set as a foundational office, it is nothing without the Chief Cornerstone. In just about every building project, one particular corner in the foundation of the building carries the load or weight of the building. The apostle is then foundational only in relation to Christ as the Chief Cornerstone.

The foundation of anything serves several purposes—security, structure and stability. How do we interpret these into layman's terms? When you think of security, you think of being protected and at peace. The apostolic office helps facilitate this in the

body of Christ through its foundational authority of

sound biblical revelation of order, structure and the security of sound doctrine of the authority of Jesus Christ. The ultimate thought is who and what do we need to be secured from or secured to? Since Jesus is the Chief Cornerstone, He ultimately secures us from the enemy and the storms of life. The apostle office, however, is set to secure us to the Chief Cornerstone, which is Jesus Christ. A weak foundation soon separates from its Chief Cornerstone, thereby allowing the whole building to be vulnerable to destruction. While others may be tricked or fooled by every wind of doctrine, the apostle office always stays firm and true to the kingdom, doctrine and ways of Jesus Christ. In the church today, we have a large falling away because of the absence of true apostles that can hold the church as a whole to sound biblical doctrine. Though we do have men with the title of apostle, many lack the right makeup to remain attached to the Chief Cornerstone.

As we think of the word *structure*, it takes on the connotation of order, legality or purpose. One of the primary responsibilities of the apostolic office is to establish and maintain order. This is established by legality, formality and purpose. In the face of legality, we must conclude that the Word of God becomes the law and prescription as to how all believers should live.

1 Corinthians 6:12 signifies that, *"All things are lawful unto me, but all things are not expedient: all things are lawful for me, but I will not be brought under the power of any."* We see the same again in 1 Corinthians 10:23 as Scripture declares, *"All things are lawful for me, but all things are not expedient: all things are lawful for me, but all things edify not."* We must understand that there are limitations to liberty in Christ. The apostolic office foundation is to help the body of Christ recognize and bring clarity to what's lawful and what's expedient. The apostle is to help clarify the purpose of the kingdom of God so that we as individuals are not brought under the power of anything contrary to the foundational truths of who Christ is in the death,

burial and resurrection that we all might be reconciled to the Father.

The apostolic office also deals with issues of formality as described in Paul's writing to the churches (Corinth, Ephesus, etc.). Paul deals with a formality issue in Romans 14:13-15. These issues seem to arise when there isn't clear instruction in the law (Word of God) to deal with specific problems at hand. That's when the apostolic office is needed the most. In some cases, the office has to offer reason with righteous resolve.

The apostolic office is constructed to be a trailblazer, one that is first to establish or attempt authority in a particular area. This is supported by 1

Corinthians 12 which indicates Jesus set the apostle first, and this is seen as the apostle went into different territories to establish the kingdom of God in the New Testament.

The validation of the apostle or the *apostellos* office has the following foundations:

o One set apart by Jesus Christ.

o One sent on a mission by Jesus Christ.

o One utilizing the Word of God as the final authority and foundation of his message.

o The office of the prophet, evangelist and pastor flow in sync with the foundational office of the apostle.

One that is a trailblazer who travels uncharted territory, evidenced by fresh ideas and areas of ministry.

- o
- o One with a robust and undeniable strength for structure and order.

- o One who brings stability, security, order, government and purpose for any work he has have been assigned.

Chapter 3
PROPHET

In this relational chapter, the prophet, it must be clear that I am going to offer an explanation concerning the office of the prophet and not the gift of prophecy. Unfortunately, a significant discrepancy exists in the body of Christ regarding this issue.

First, let's look at several basic definitions of a prophet in relation to the office and how it relates to the governmental structure of God's church.

The *American Heritage Dictionary of Cultural Literacy, Third Edition* indicates that a prophet is *someone who brings a message from God to people; its general usage is someone who can foretell the future.*

Random House Unabridged Dictionary interprets a prophet as *a person who speaks by divine inspiration or as the interpreter through whom the will of God is expressed, a person gifted with profound moral insight and exceptional powers of expression, a predictor, a soothsayer.*

Strong's Concordance indicates that the Greek word for prophet is *prophetuo*—which means *to foretell events, divine, speak under inspiration, exercise the prophetic office.*

Examining these definitions, we see a common thread being used to define a prophet as one who foretells the future. This means that a prophet is one who takes what has not yet been revealed, seen or discussed and brings it forth. However, *Strong's* Greek interpretation goes further by explaining that a prophet must fulfill the prophetic office and not prophesy alone.

The English word *office* signifies a context of a formal, authoritative structure. In relation to our definition as well as the biblical history of this office, we can conclude that there is an authoritative structure concerning the prophet.

The office of prophet is indeed the second office Jesus set for His church according to 1 Corinthians 12:28, when we equate the act of Jesus setting offices for the establishment of His church. We can look at the process of a builder equipping a building for use. The first thing that is laid is the foundation, which is the apostle. Secondly, the frame of the building is placed. It's ironic that when a building is complete, the only thing that is visible is the walls, *i.e.,* the frame. The foundation of any building is not necessarily visible because that's not its purpose. However, the full intent of the office of the prophet is to be an interpreter through which the will of God is expressed (*Random Dictionary*).

The Old Testament prophet indeed went beyond what we call the first level of prophecy, which is merely revealing the unseen. Amos 3:7 declares that

God will not do anything unless He reveals it to His servants, the prophets; true prophets embody the Word of God in their lives and actions. They also set forth standards of righteousness as declared in the Word.

The Prophet Jonah is an example. In Jonah 1:1, Jonah received a word from God and ultimately delivered that word to the people of Nineveh. The word was one of correction and warning to effect change. The same was true of Nathan and David in II Samuel 12:2-7; Nathan, being a prophet of the Lord, also brought correction by prophetic revelation.

What gives the office of prophet authority to act in

such a manner—different from one that walks

in the gift of prophecy—is that the one that sits in the office of the prophet flows in the prophetic continually. We come to understand that the office of the prophet is set as part of the structure, solely based on its position with the foundation and Chief Cornerstone, while the one that walks in the gift of prophecy is specifically for the flow within the structure of God's church.

Governmentally, the prophet also has the responsibility of assuring the relational structure is framed well by enforcing the obedient order of God to the church. Generally, when God spoke to a prophet, it was to move the people into a realm of obedience.

Chapter 4
EVANGELIST

The office of evangelist through our time has been overlooked and misrepresented within the Christian church. Denominations within the Protestant church all relate to the office of the evangelist differently.

The Greek Lexicon gives the Aramaic word for evangelist as *euanggelion* as used in the Canonic titles of the four Gospels, meaning *a reward for good news given to the messenger; (eu) meaning good; to bring a message; good news.* The latter terms give rise to the word *gospel.*

Strong's Concordance gives the word *evangelist* as *a preacher of the gospel* and comes from *evaggelizo: to announce good news.*

The word *evangelist* is found three times in the New Testament; from our previous Greek definition, we can see that an evangelist is one who tells the good news or gives a proclamation of the gospel.

The verb form of the same word is used fifty-five times in the New Testament and is usually translated as the equivalent of the separate Greek phrase *preach the gospel,* which is found eleven times. A comparison of the two lists shows that Luke and Paul preferred the word *evangelize,* whereas Matthew and Mark gave

preference to the phrase *preach the gospel.* A careful

examination of these passages reveals that an evangelist and a preacher of the gospel, biblically speaking, is the same thing, with the word *evangelize* emphasizing the joyous nature of the message, and the word *preach* referring to the public nature of the proclamation. An evangelist is one who publicly demonstrates the news of the gospel.

In fact, when we examine the offices of the structural establishment of the kingdom (or God's government), the evangelist is the only one that has a responsibility to those outside the church itself. Since that is the case, we can safely determine that the office of the evangelist acts more in the form of public relations for the governing of God. Typically,

we see

that the rise and fall of the church to the public eye has been based on the performance or lack of performance via the multiple evangelists. For instance, in most cases if there is a potential scandal brewing within the church with a pastor or elder, the world typically has no response to that. But if an evangelist, whose primary focus is reaching out to the "unchurched," has some issue brewing, that would likely be on the ten o'clock news.

We can also see that manifested in another form. If a local church were doing great things in the community or with its members, it's unlikely the world would know anything about it. However, if an evangelist were operating publicly, as evangelists should, doing great things of the kingdom, he would more than likely catch the eye of local officials who want to get in on the activities.

I give great respect and honor to evangelists because, out of all of the offices, they have what I would call a twofold position. Not only are they agents in expanding the kingdom, but they also act as a report to the things that are outside of the kingdom perspective. In 2 Timothy 4:5, when Paul instructed Timothy to do the work of an evangelist, we must ask what Paul was governmentally asking Timothy to perform? 2 Timothy 4:2 gives us insight into what Paul was encouraging Timothy to do. He advised

him to preach the word, be instant in season and
out,

reprove, rebuke and exhort with *doctrine* (kingdom principles). Verse 5 says to watch all things and endure afflictions.

When you look at afflictions, what comes to mind is an outside source attempting to harbor or bring pain. Paul tells Timothy that, as a part of doing the work of an evangelist, he is to stand against the attack of the enemy against the kingdom to destroy it. Paul specifically instructs Timothy to endure these afflictions. This reinforces the thought that the office of evangelist is the extended architectural arm of God's government to those that don't believe. We must remember that the Word of God that the evangelist brings to the world is indeed good news, but at the same time, it is a two-edged sword.

The miraculous gifts were needed to authenticate the gospel message at a time of new revelatory activity (Exodus 4:5, 1 Kings 17:4, John 10:25, 2 Corinthians 12:12, etc.)—during the foundation-laying period of the church.

Chapter 5

PASTOR

A reoccurring question in the body of Christ seems to be, *Who or what is a pastor?* Another frequent question is *What is the pastor's official roll in the governing structure of God's kingdom?* Throughout history, we have seen pastors take on the primary role of running our local churches. We have also seen them become the major focal point within the relationship of the other offices, *i.e.,* apostle, prophet, evangelist. Scripture clearly shows us that Jesus has truly given the office of pastor to help Him govern His body. Jeremiah 3:15 says that He (God) will give us pastors according to His heart who will feed us with

knowledge and

understanding. This is God's way to have direct contact with His body, just as many politicians have local offices to reach out to their constituents. Pastors help illustrate Christ's full authority concerning the order of God. Out of all the offices mentioned, the pastor and the prophet are the only ones mentioned in the Old Testament.

The language used in Jeremiah 3:15 can be misleading if not read in context. For instance, the word *give,* in *Strong's Concordance* is *Nathan,* which in the Hebrew means *to put, make, add, apply or appoint.* Therefore we have to incorporate the office of pastor as a set structure in God's government, again differing from the thought in Ephesians 4:11 where

God uses

the thought of giving a gift to the body of Christ. This gives us clarity that there is also the office of pastor that is set to operate as the heart of God to the body, delivering knowledge and bringing understanding.

In the building structure, we can declare that the pastor becomes the mortar, supplying strength and unity amongst the other offices. This does not make the pastor greater than the other offices; it's merely the position that God has placed in the office.

Let's examine what God intended for the office of pastor to provide. The first, outlined in Jeremiah 3:15, is that the pastor is to feed the people with knowledge and understanding. Let's look at the definition of each:

Knowledge: the sum or range of what has been perceived, discovered or learned; familiarity, awareness gained through experience or study

Understanding: the quality of one who understands; comprehension, individual or specified judgment or outlook; opinion

The governmental office of the pastor is to bring knowledge to the body of Christ. Many assert that the pastor role is actually that of pastor/teacher. I believe the pastor's office in the body of Christ goes beyond merely teaching the Bible. The Scripture declares God will give pastors that will feed His children with knowledge, but it doesn't specifically limit that to Bible knowledge. The pastor's office is what could be termed a life coach position, established by God through His divine knowledge to impart information and a godly standard of living, facilitating a discovered and learned perception of God's government and promises for the believer. The information received should become familiar, and each believer should become aware of the knowledge gained through his own personal experience and study.

As we have seen, the pastor is to bring understanding as well. It becomes ironic that God uses the word *knowledge* before using the word *understanding*. God considers understanding to be essential; Proverbs 4:5 says, *"Get wisdom, get understanding."* Verse 7 of the same chapter says, *"Wisdom is the principal thing; therefore, get wisdom: and with all thy getting get understanding."* God's intention for the body of Christ, who is subject to His throne, is for us to understand His government through the process of receiving His knowledge as described earlier. Proverbs 3:5 exhorts us to, *"Trust in the Lord with all thine heart; and lean not unto thine own understanding."* He shows us that in order to understand the knowledge received and His governments (His order, His ways), you can't trust

your own level of understanding; you

will gain that understanding only through His level of understanding. The fascinating thing about this is that God's government was intended for all humanity, to assist them in becoming the best they could be and live in the established peace of His will. Unfortunately, this intent has been reduced in man's eyes to apply only to those that believe. However, the fact is that when the appointed time comes, we all will have knowledge of the authority of Jesus Christ and His ruling power as He sits at the right hand of God the Father on His throne, making intercession for those that do believe. Everyone, believer or not, will then understand that He is God and will have no other gods before Him. (See Exodus 20:2-3.)

Chapter 6

WHY RESTORATION?

The biblical meaning of the word *restoration* is *to receive back more than has been lost to the point where the final state is greater than the original condition.* The main point is that someone or something is improved beyond measure. Unlike the dictionary definition of restoration, which is *to return something to its original condition,* the biblical definition of the word has greater connotations that go above and beyond the typical everyday usage. Repeatedly throughout the Bible, God blesses people for their faith and hardships by making up for their losses and giving them more than they had previously.

> *Brethren, if a man be overtaken in a fault, ye which are spiritual, restore such an one in the spirit of meekness; considering thyself, lest thou also be tempted. Bear ye one another's burdens, and so fulfill the law of Christ. For if a man think himself to be something, when he is nothing, he deceiveth himself.* (Galatians 6:1-3, KJV)

What is the qualifier for someone to restore you? The first qualifier we see is that one must be **spiritual**, coming from the Greek word *pneumatikos*, which means *relating to the human spirit, or rational soul,* *as part of the man which is akin to God and serves as His*

instrument or

organ, that which possesses the nature of the rational soul,

belonging to a spirit, or a being higher than man but inferior

to God, belonging to the Divine Spirit, of God the Holy

Spirit, one who is filled with and governed by the Spirit of

God, pertaining to the wind or breath; windy, exposed to the

wind, blowing.

The second qualifier is **meekness** coming from

the Greek *praotēs,* meaning *gentleness, mildness, meekness.*

It's also important that we understand the meaning

of the word *fault* as it is used in this passage. Coming

from the Greek *paraptōma,* it means *to fall beside or near*

something, a lapse or deviation from truth and uprightness, a

sin.

Paraptōma comes from the word *parapiptō* which means *to fall beside a person or thing, to slip aside, to deviate from the right path, turn aside, wander, to error, to fall away (from the true faith): from worship of Jehovah which comes from the root word* piptō *which means to descend from a higher place to a lower, to fall (either from or upon), to be thrust down, to descend from an erect to a prostrate position, of those overcome by terror or astonishment or grief or under the attack of an evil spirit or of falling dead suddenly, to be cast down from a state of prosperity, to fall from a state of uprightness, to lose authority, no longer have force.*

One of the most needed and yet most neglected ministries in the body of Christ is that

**of going after and seeking to restore a
brother or sister who has been overtaken in a
fault.**

The ministry of restoration belongs to all who are
spiritual, which means spiritually mature—those who
walk in the Spirit.

*16 So I say, walk by the Spirit, and you will not gratify the
desires of the flesh. 17 For the flesh desires what is contrary to
the Spirit, and the Spirit what is contrary to the flesh. They
are in conflict with each other so that you are not to do
whatever you want. 18 But if you are led by the Spirit, you are
not under the law. 19 The acts of the flesh are obvious: sexual*

immorality, impurity, and debauchery; [20] *idolatry and witchcraft; hatred, discord, jealousy, fits of rage, selfish ambition, dissensions, factions* [21] *and envy;*

drunkenness, orgies, and the like. I warn you, as I

did before, that those who live like this will not

inherit the kingdom of God. [22] *But the fruit of the*

Spirit is love, joy, peace, forbearance, kindness,

goodness, faithfulness, [23] *gentleness, and self-*

control. Against such things, there is no law.

[24] *Those who belong to Christ Jesus have crucified*

the flesh with its passions and desires. [25] *Since we*

live by the Spirit, let us keep in step with the

Spirit. [26] *Let us not become conceited, provoking*

and envying each other. (Galatians 5:16-26,

NIV)

You will notice that the Scripture doesn't say that

those who are spiritual are necessarily those that

possess and hold a title, position or office. It's not the office that needs to be restored or healed; it's the person—the man, the woman. Many times, we focus on restoring people to some position/title/office they might have lost instead of restoring them to their position as a child of God. Real restoration must be done outside the confines of the office in which someone walks. God is after the substance of the heart, and sometimes the robes of bishop, apostle, prophet, pastor and teacher get in the way. Those who refuse to receive personal help and healing because they fear losing their position should consider whether they are truly called to that office in the first place.

A person needing restoration must recognize the initial phase of a fault. When you're in this position, the first step of recognition is to see the **gates** that have been opened in your life.

> *Keep thy heart with all diligence; for out of it are the issues of life.* (Proverbs 4:23, KJV)

> *A good man out of the good treasure of his heart bringeth forth that which is good; and an evil man out of the evil treasure of his heart bringeth forth that which is evil: for of the abundance of the heart, his mouth speaketh.* (Luke 6:45, KJV)

It is also important to understand **offenses.**

*¹ Then said he unto the disciples, it is impossible but that offenses will come: but woe unto him, through whom they come! ² It were better for him that a millstone were hanged about his neck, and he cast into the sea than that he should offend one of these little ones. ³ Take heed to yourselves: If thy brother trespass against thee, **rebuke** him; and if he repent, forgive him. ⁴ And if he trespass against thee seven times in a day, and seven times in a day turn again to thee, saying, I repent; thou shalt forgive him. ⁵ And the apostles said unto the Lord, Increase our faith.* (Luke 17:1-5, KJV)

Another major contributor to being overtaken in a fault is a failure to deal with hurt. The adage that "hurt people hurt people" is so true and relevant when it comes to leaders in the body of Christ. When leaders do not deal with their hurt and pain, it spreads like cancer to the laity they serve and ultimately the full body, whether local or global.

Initially, you must identify the seed. "What you feed leads." Whatever you spend time feeding ultimately identifies the character in what and how you lead.

Peace I leave with you; my peace I give to you. Not as the world gives do I give to you. Let not your hearts be troubled, neither let them be afraid. (John 14:27, ESV)

Love bears all things, believes all things, hopes all things, endures all things. (1 Corinthians 13:7, ESV)

One of the major issues plaguing leaders and restoration is that we often want to forego the process. I say don't ignore the process. It becomes essential for the one being restored to adhere to the full process of restoration; avoid the temptation to decide you are better and then to make the mistake of returning to full activity too soon. Restoration is not an overnight process. Just like you should finish all the medicine the doctor prescribes for an infection and not stop taking it just because you feel

a little

better, you shouldn't cut short the time spent in the restoration process either.

And be not conformed to this world: but be ye transformed by the renewing of your mind, that ye may prove what is that good, and acceptable, and perfect, will of God. (Romans 12:2, KJV)

Making our minds new again is a challenging but much-needed process to respect and honor for full restoration to take place in our lives. It is also necessary that you not be identified by your fault or issue. Don't allow your pain to be your identity. Note Psalm 23:3 (ESV): *He restores my soul. He leads me in paths of righteousness for his name's sake.* If your soul is not part of the healing equation in your restoration, you will continuously see yourself and identify yourself with your fault, and so will others. Most people see you as you see yourself. In the soul being restored, the mind, will, intellect and emotions all need to experience restoration and healing.

Chapter 7

THE HEART OF THE MATTER

Understanding government is a daunting task. From the definitions discussed so far, we see that Jesus is the continuous authority exercising the order of God over His Kingdom as a prevailing prince. For one to have a government in place is merely their way to govern men. 1 Corinthians 10:26 tell us, *"For the earth is the Lord's, and the fullness thereof,"* and it becomes relevant that we, being on the earth, should submit to God's governing righteousness. We find in Genesis 2:7 that God created man in His image, formed us from the dust (earth) of the ground, blew into us (we became full), then we became a living

soul.

God's governmental authority becomes even more relevant when we look to the death, burial and resurrection of Christ. On the cross, Jesus was the Lamb without spot carrying the sin of man on his shoulders. This is type and shadow of Isaiah 9:6a which says, *"For unto us a child is born, unto us a son is given."* Jesus was the child born unto us, with Mary being the surrogate for His birth; and He was also the Son given by God the Father. Uniquely, Jesus being God, He had to also enter the common world to legally be able to take authority. In most governments, a person can't represent a people unless they also reside in the same location or they are from the same people acting as an ambassador.

Jesus followed

through with being the suitable sacrifice to cleanse mankind of sin. He died on the cross but rose again with all authority in His hand, which legally reunited the heavens and the earth under His new throne.

1 Corinthians 12:28 becomes His signature for how His government would be established, and Ephesians 4:11 defines how His government will function in the earth. 1 Corinthians 12:4 tells us that there are diversities of gifts, but the same Spirit, and 1 Corinthians 12:11 says that all the gifts work by the same Spirit (Jesus), but He divides severally to every man as he will.

Ephesians 4:11 also defines what we have come to

know as the fivefold ministry gifts, again differing

from 1 Corinthians 12:28. The description of the title names may be the same, but they differ in purpose and function. 1 Corinthians 12:28 was purposed to structure God's kingdom in the earth, and Ephesians 4:11 deals with gifts being given to the body of Christ as a part of God's government to perfect one another so that we all can work in the ministry to bring about the edification of the body of Christ.

By the Spirit of adoption, we all become ministers (servants). We are our brother's keeper, and we now have the privilege and responsibility to walk in the anointing and gifting that God has given us. As a believer and a member of Christ's cabinet, we must become apostolic in view, giving precedence to the gospel as the foundation for everyday life. We must also become prophetic by *speaking those things that be not as though they were,* declaring the Word of God in our own lives as well as the lives of our family and friends; exemplifying the growth of the kingdom by spreading the good news of Jesus Christ to every man and fulfilling the Great Commission; bringing to life 1 Corinthians 13, showing forth the love we seek from pastors to the wounded and broken soldier; and, finally, walking as Timothy did and teaching the Word of God by the Spirit, experience and intellectual stimulation while putting every believer in remembrance of God's Word.

www.ingramcontent.com/pod-product-compliance
Lightning Source LLC
Chambersburg PA
CBHW031627040426
42452CB00007B/717